THOUGHTS TO HEAL

The Shri Guru Granth Sahib Way

© KAWALJIT SINGH BHATIA

Preface

We as humans are unique compared to other species. What makes us unique is our ability to think, reflect and look at things from an intellectual point of view. In fact, the way we think has a huge impact on your lives. As a kid our thought process is very clear – to grow up, be independent and have a great life. But as we start growing, we are bombarded with conflicting thoughts. Our parameters of contentment, which once were limited to small and meaningful things, like love, care and attention, shift to materialistic and expensive things like watches, cars, etc.

I am not for a moment suggesting that there is anything wrong in possessing materialistic things; but yes, one should not base his happiness and contentment on such things. It is only if one is self-sufficient that one can help others. But in our journey to be self-sufficient, we get greedy. The joy of giving is forgotten and we make our lives miserable by depending upon such things for happiness which can never give us happiness. Our life becomes like a ship lost on high seas without a compass, not knowing what to do or where to go.

In such a situation, we start working on an auto-pilot mode. Instead of taking conscious decisions and actions, we merely react to situations. We work because we have to meet deadlines or have to earn money, not because we love the work we do; we exercise because we need to look good, not because we want to lead a healthy life; we pray so that things start happening the way we want them to be, not out of a heartfelt love, awe and gratitude for our Creator. Hence, even the good things that we do are for a temporary period, because the thought behind doing it not deep, good or earnest enough.

If you feel that your thought-process is all jumbled and you do not know whether you are doing the right thing or the things that matter, this book is for you. This book contains some teachings from Shri Guru Granth Sahib Ji (SGGS) and is intended to reinvigorate your thought process so that you can put your life and actions in perspective.

SGGS, which is the Holy Scripture and also the 11th Guru for Sikhs, is a unique scripture. What makes SGGS unique is that though being a religious scripture, SGGS is not confined to teachings of the Sikh Gurus alone. SGGS contains teachings of various saints from other religions as well. The followers of Sikhism are called *Sikhs*, meaning Disciple/ Student. In Sikh religion the importance of knowledge (*Gyan*) is very high. It is considered that knowledge is something which knows no barriers and transcends all religions. In kneeling before the SGGS, the Sikhs not only kneel before the 11th Guru, but also the words of wisdom contained therein.

The present book contains a few teachings from SGGS. The 31 chapters that this book contains is to be read and applied one by one each day. By doing so, you will see a sea change in the way you perceive things. As a result, the quality of your life is bound to improve. You will feel much lighter in the heart and clearer in the head. Happiness will follow you. I give you *Thoughts to Heal* with a prayer that you may find that missing link to your happiness hidden somewhere in this book, so that you may experience everlasting happiness and contentment in your life. God bless!

Acknowledgements

I would like to thank the Almighty for this life - with its ups and downs, a lovely family, wonderful experiences and everything else, that He has given me.

I would also like to thank my family, especially my parents, for their ceaseless sacrifices and endless efforts, to raise me as a good human being. It is from them that I learnt that life is not only about receiving, but also about giving.

I would also like to thank my lovely wife for filling my life with love, happiness and laughter. It is from her that I learnt that one needs to have a simple thought-process and honest approach to find everlasting happiness in life.

I would finally like to thank Harji conversations with whom are always enriching. Without the love and support of these people, I could not have written this book.

1.

Bin Boojhay Karam Kamaavnay Janam Padaarath Kho-Ay

"To act without understanding is to lose the treasure of this human life"

(Ang 33)

Knowing is one thing and realisation is another. Most of us live through our lives in a reactive mode, without putting in thoughts to our actions. Our actions in fact are mere reactions to the situations, instead of being a conscious action, based on our belief and value systems. We keep moving through life with the crowd, feeling comfortable that we have company. We were born alone and in death we shall be alone. So do not be afraid to be alone, especially when you have to realise yourself and do what you were meant to do. Everyone has a unique purpose. Generating money has become the only driving force, with no attention to much more important things in life, like happiness, family, etc. We think, one fine day everything shall be alright. Many lives have finished waiting for that one fine day to arrive. Does what you do give you happiness? If not, think of what would give you happiness and what is stopping you from doing it? Life is the scarcest resource that you have. Hence treat it like a treasure. Sri Guru Granth Sahib Ji advises us to put thoughts into our actions, for its realisation alone that distinguishes humans from animals. Once you know what makes you happy, move towards it. The purpose of every human being is different, that's why what gives happiness to a person may appear dull to another. Live your life in realisation.

2.

Jayhaa Beejai So Lunai Karmaa Sand-
Rhaa Khayt
*"As she has planted, so does she
harvest; such is the field of
karma."*

(Ang 134)

One thing that one cannot erase or
change is Karma. Whatever is done is
done for ever. One can of course do
better karma and reduce the bad
karma. But a good or bad deed once
done is done forever. It's like placing a
longer string beside a string to make
it shorter. Whether you believe in

Karma or not, one thing is for sure, a good deed makes us feel good. And a person with a good feeling can do wonders. He/ she is an asset to people around himself or herself. Everyone likes to be around someone positive and hence good things start happening to such positive people. Since good karma helps one grow in positivity, it leads to such people being sought after. That is one way to look at karma. Let's look at it another way. When we do good, the person to whom good is done starts believing in the power of doing good, because he or she shall forever be grateful for the good you have done to them. Similar acts by a fairly large number of people imbibes a sense of goodness in the society. When we all become good, there no room for the bad. So it's in our own interest to do and propagate good.

Sikh Gurus always stressed in goodness of action. Be it through seva (service), dasvand (donating a tenth of your earning to charity or langar) or through protecting the underprivileged, because good always begets good. Guru Gobind Singh ji is the only person in history who won many wars, but never conquered an inch of land. Why? Because the wars were fought to protect the oppressed from a tyrannical empire which was resorting to forceful conversion. And the oppressed masses were not Sikhs. Yet He was always willing to do anything to sacrifice everything He had for anyone who came to Him for protection. He sacrificed His family and His life to protect the oppressed masses. He taught His Sikhs to believe in goodness of actions and to forever stand up for what is right.

You can't change the world, but you can definitely change yourself, and that may change the world in some way. Shri Guru Granth Sahib Ji teaches us to believe in good actions and do them to be in a position to beget good. So be good and you shall see how the world around you changes.

3.

Ik-Onkaar Satgur Parsaad.

Bandnaa Har Bandnaa Gun Gaavhu
Gopaal Raa-Ay.

"One Universal Creator God. By The
Grace Of The True Guru:
I bow in reverence to the Lord, I bow
in reverence. I sing the Glorious
Praises of the Lord, my King."

(Ang 683)

Surrender yourself to the will of God.
He will look after you. Most of us
think that we have control over
everything, and get irritated when

things start slipping out of our hands. Come to think of it, what if the Earth stops spinning someday, what if a comet hits the Earth, but does it? God has created this Universe and He is the one who runs it according to His plan. Surrender to His will. Life will be a lot easier. But do not be complacent. The message is to put in your best and after you have done that, smile, because after you have genuinely put in all the hard work, you are in God's hands. The outcome will be according to His will and His will is always the best for you, though in the short term, it may appear otherwise. So stop worrying and start believing.

4.

Javayhay karam kamaavdaa tavayhay faltay.

"According to the deeds which one does, so are the fruits one obtains."

(Ang 317)

The focus should be on good deeds. The more good deeds you do unto others, the better poised you are to receive good, from the person you have been good to and from others. If for nothing else, just for your peace of mind, be good to others. At times it so happens that we receive help from unknown quarters. It's like finding money is some forgotten pocket. The good that you do, ultimately does come back to you, immediately or later. So believe in the power of goodness and keep doing good.

Once an 18-year-old student was struggling to pay his fees. He was an orphan, and not knowing where to turn for money, he came up with a bright idea. He and a friend decided to host a musical concert on campus to raise money for their education. They reached out to the great pianist Ignacy J. Paderewski. His manager demanded a guaranteed fee of $2000 for the piano recital. A deal was struck and the boys began to work to make the concert a success.

The big day arrived. But unfortunately, they had not managed to sell enough tickets. The total collection was only $1600. Disappointed, they went to Paderewski and explained their plight. They gave him the entire $1600, plus a cheque for the balance $400. They promised to honour the cheque at the soonest possible.

"No," said Paderewski. "This is not acceptable." He tore up the cheque, returned the $1600 and told the two boys: "Here's the $1600. Please deduct whatever expenses you have incurred. Keep the money you need for your fees. And just give me whatever is left". The boys were surprised, and thanked him profusely. It was a small act of kindness. But it clearly marked out Paderewski as a great human being.

Paderewski later went on to become the Prime Minister of Poland. He was a great leader, but unfortunately when the World War began, Poland was ravaged. There were more than 1.5 million people starving in his country, and no money to feed them. Paderewski did not know where to turn for help. He reached out to the

US Food and Relief Administration for help. The head there was a man called Herbert Hoover who later went on to become the US President. Hoover agreed to help and quickly shipped tons of food grains to feed the starving Polish people.

A calamity was averted. Paderewski was relieved. He decided to go across to meet Hoover and personally thank him. When Paderewski began to thank Hoover for his noble gesture, Hoover quickly interjected and said, "You shouldn't be thanking me Mr. Prime Minister. You may not remember this, but several years ago, you helped two young students go through college. I was one of them."

Have you sown the seeds of your good actions yet?

5

Har Sangi Raate Mitai Sabh Chintaa

"When attuned to God, one is free of all worry"

(Ang 201)

The Almighty is a power, which is unparalleled. The good, bad and the ugly are all his creations. His plans are meticulous for us, it's for our limited understanding that we cannot fathom His designs. So stop worrying and get connected to the ultimate powerhouse of the Universe. Before starting any work, take His name and put in all your hard work with utmost sincerity and dedication. Nothing in this world can stop you then. You become unstoppable! When you look back, everything makes sense. Isn't it? So the bad phase that you are in will also come to pass. Everything will make sense, in a couple of days, months or years from now. Just keep your faith as of now and keep moving.

I would like to share a real life story. Once an old lady was walking towards an ATM to withdraw some money. While she was walking down she was doing *Simran* (chanting God's name) with a string of beads in her hand. She saw two huge men approaching her from the opposite direction in a suspicious manner. She sensed danger and got scared but continued the *Simran.* She tightly gripped her bag and held it close to herself. Just as they got very near to her they suddenly looked confused and parted and made way for her to walk between them. They just crossed her without any harm. The old woman was relieved. She smiled about the stupid thought that came to her head.

The very next day, the old lady got a phone call from the police station and is called for some interrogation. When she reached the police station, she is shocked to find the two huge men also present there. The police officer tells her that they saw her in the

CCTV footage near the ATM where another woman had been robbed and tracked her down from the ATM transaction records. They were surprised to see in the CCTV footage that while the robbers approached the old lady to rob her, they suddenly seemed to change their mind and later attack another woman. The two huge men were asked to see the CCTV footage and asked them why didn't they attack the old lady when she was an easy target. They said, though it's not visible in the CCTV footage, but when they approached the old woman for robbing her, two bodyguards appeared from nowhere and started walking behind her. Seeing them they got scared and decided not to rob her but someone else. When the police asked the old lady whether she had any bodyguards, she said she had none. No one had an answer to this. This the old lady now maintains, were God sent angels whom the God had sent to protect her.

So keep the faith and keep moving. Be fearless and you shall be unstoppable. The Supreme Force is behind you if you believe in Him.

6.

Ho-ay Pavitar Sareer

Charnaa Dhooree-ai.

Paarbarahm Gurdayv Sadaa Hajooree-

ai.

"My body is sanctified, by the dust of

Your feet.

O Supreme Lord God, Divine Guru,

You are always with me, ever-present."

(Ang 709)

The Gurus in Sikh faith are a part of

the Almighty. Whoever you believe in,

God, Allah, Ishwar, they are names of

the One and the same God. Only

colour of your vision changes by the

colour of your glasses, not the object. What you would be seeing remains unchanged by the colour of your glass. Likewise it is the same God in different religions. Just the manifestations are different based on different cultures, regions, practices, dietary habits, etc. God only made humans, its humans who made religions. Surrender yourself and dedicate all your actions and deeds to that Almighty. The only thing that your heart should ever desire is His company and blessings.

As the story goes, both Arjuna and Duryodhana had gone to Lord Krishna to seek help for the war at

Kurukshetra, which is now known as Mahabharata. Lord Krishna's army was the Narayani Sena, which could never be defeated. But Lord Krishna could give the army to only one person, either Arjuna or Duryodhana. When asked, Arjuna without wasting a second chose Lord Krishna over the invincible army. Duryodhana was happy with the army, since he had come there to request for the unconquerable army. Rest we all know how Lord Krishna ensured that the Pandavas won, even when Arjuna did not want to be a part of the war.

God knows what we want and He ensures we get what we deserve.

Hence, the only thing that one should desire is the Almighty's grace and blessings. Rest all follows. When you are in His hands, you are in the safest place in the Universe and nothing can harm you

Usṭaṭ Nindaa Kis Kee Keejai.

Cheenahu Aap Japahu Jagdeesar
Har Jagannaath Man Bhaa-I-Aa.
"Who does he praise or slander?
Know yourself, and meditate on
the Lord of the Universe; let
your mind be pleased with the
Lord, the Master of the
Universe."

(Ang 1041)

Do not waste your time and energy in

discussing, especially ill, about

people. The scarcest resource in this

universe is your life, everything else

will recycle itself. But your life is getting lesser breath by breath. The time left on this Earth that you have today is lesser than that you had yesterday. Would you want to waste such valuable gift on discussing people or in improving yourself? Every person has something good in himself or herself. Even the worst of people may be very talented – it is just a matter of unveiling and discovering yourself. You yourself are a beautiful creation God. Hold yourself in high esteem. Take care of yourself and in doing so thank Him for giving you such a beautiful body which is a sanctuary for your soul.

So, instead of discussing people, start building on self.

Kabeer Garab Na Keejee-Ai Rank Na
Hasee-Ai Ko-Ay.
Ajahu So Naa-O Samundar Meh Ki-
Aa Jaan-O Ki-Aa Ho-Ay.

"Kabeer, do not be so proud,
and do not laugh at the poor.
Your boat is still out at sea; who
knows what will happen?"

(Ang 1366)

Even the greatest have had a fall.
Pride, arrogance, vanity numbs the
senses. Things that make us human
can be felt no more. Be a human
being first, because that is one race
common to all mankind. What makes
us human are feelings of compassion

and empathy towards fellow human beings. A weak or a vulnerable person will not stay so forever. Winners know this and start making valued relationships early in life. Always be genuinely good to everyone around you. Arrogance and haughty attitude may get the job done in the short run, but in the long run, you have no one beside you. Be happy in the happiness of others and a strong pillar of support in times of their loss. The whole world will then be a family. It will be a win-win situation for all. An arrogant person loses people in his life by the second. It may help him/ her get past here and there but will surely lead him/ her to his/ her fall.

9.

Toon Gur Pitaa Toon Hai Gur
Maataa Toon Gur Ban Dhap Mayraa
Sakhaa Sakhaa-Ay.
*"O Guru, You are my father. O
Guru, You are my mother. O
Guru, You are my relative,
companion and friend."*

(Ang 167)

This line is like a cure for the broken heart and a tired soul. In today's fast life, it is possible to get burnt out easily and feel dejected. Repeat this line in your head at least 5 times and feel that the Almighty is with you, standing like a pillar of support

behind you and you are telling this to Him. It will work like magic on you. When all is lost, keep the faith and you shall regain everything, more than what you might have lost. When you have the Almighty by your side, there is nothing to worry about at all.

10

Puhap Ma<u>dh</u> Ji-O Baas Basa<u>t</u> Hai

Mukar Maahi Jaisay <u>Chh</u>aa-Ee.

<u>T</u>aisay Hee Har Basay Nira<u>nt</u>ar <u>Gh</u>at

Hee <u>Kh</u>ojahu <u>Bh</u>aa-Ee.

"Like the fragrance which
remains in the flower, and like
the reflection in the mirror,

The Lord dwells deep within;
search for Him within your own
heart, O Siblings of Destiny."

(Ang 684)

The power of the Universe lies within you. Whatever you can think of, you can achieve. Whatever you seek, the power to achieve it lies within you. We

look for approval from others when the unique contribution that we can make is probably that no one else can make. If a tiger starts wanting to be loved like a pet dog, it will never be able to unearth its true potential. In the effort, it will neither become a dog, nor remain a tiger. Whenever you try to look for reasons, things, happiness, etc. outside, you start wandering.

Once a crow, relaxing at the edge of a field saw a herd of sheep grazing. Suddenly, an eagle swooped from nowhere and grabbed a lamb by its neck and the very next moment disappeared into the blue sky. The crow was impressed by what it saw and felt like doing the same. So like an eagle, it flew as high as it could and started circling the sky. It saw a herd of buffalos grazing. Seeing a small calf, it swooped on it and tried to pick it up. But its claws got stuck in the calf's skin. The shepherd saw the crow and quickly killed it. So who was responsible for such a tragic end of the crow? The shepherd – No, the calf – no, the eagle – no. It was the crow itself which was responsible because it tried to be something it was not and in doing so, it tried to exactly copy the eagle. Do not kill yourself in trying to be someone else.

Stop your outwardly search and start your journey from within, starting today. Whatever be it, you can achieve it – all that is required is a genuine effort from within.

Saath Na Chaalai Bin Bhajan Bikhi-
Aa Saglee Chhaar.
Har Har Naam Kamaavanaa Naanak
Ih Dhan Saar.

*"Nothing shall go along with
you, except your devotion. All
corruption is like ashes.*

*Practice the Name of the Lord,
Har, Har. O Nanak, this is the
most excellent wealth."*

(Ang 228)

Life is what happens to us between
being dust. The lowly earth gets a
chance to manifest into a beautiful

human form by the grace of God, so use this precious form to thank the Almighty and to sing His praises. This will give you inner strength to fight everyday troubles. The work that you do, the money that you generate, you, are all temporary - they come and go. But the time that you spend in God's contemplation stays with you. You take that to your grave. So do spend some time during the day to meditate on God, and feel the inner peace.

Jay Aa̱tam Ka-O

Su̱kh Su̱kh Ni̱t Lo̱rhahu Ṯaan Sa̱tgur

Saran Paveejai.

*"If you long for everlasting
peace and comfort for your
soul, then enter the Sanctuary
of the True Guru."*

(Ang 1326)

There is no dearth in God's house.
There is enough for everyone, every
time. You may have loads of wealth,
but you may not find it sufficient to
keep you happy. That is because deep
down, your soul knows that
materialistic wealth is not the true
wealth. Meditate in God's name, the

true wealth, and you shall

contentment. It is by cons

keeping your Creator in you

thoughts that you derive emotional

and mental strength. You develop an

attitude of abundance, because the

focus shifts from receiving to giving.

So, for you inner peace, be one with

God. Speak to Him, enter his

Sanctuary.

Sabh Ayk Darisat
Samat Kar Daykhai Sabh Aatam
Raam Pachhaan Jee-O.

Har Har Jas Gaa-I-Aa Param
Pad Paa-I-Aa Tay Ootam Jan
Pardhaan Jee-O.

*"They look upon all with
equality, and recognize the
Supreme Soul, the Lord,
pervading among all.*

*Those who sing the Praises of
the Lord, Har, Har, obtain the
supreme status; they are the
most exalted and acclaimed
people."*

The spiritual ones treat everyone with equality, because they know that it is one soul of the universe that is running through everyone. The ones who are out there to divide people in the name of religion are not spiritual at all in the true sense. Nature may manifest itself in diverse forms by giving everyone and every specie a different appearance. But taken collectively, we are all one big family. The difference between human beings is because of the manmade parameters on which everyone is judged. If you do not drink water, you will die; if you get assaulted, you will feel the pain; if you feel sad, you will cry – it's not different for the rich or the poor. Hence everyone is equal. Yet, the moment we are born, we 'are given' an identity. This identity is temporary identity, which will come to an end with your death. The identity given by the Giver is that of a human being, the prime one amongst all His creations. Let's live up to the identity given by Him. Enough bad things have been done in the name of religion. Religion is man-made, but a human is made by God. Let's look at the human being beyond religion, skin colour, language and barriers. Let's be the children of the One

Almighty. Let's be one big family and treat everyone like our family members. Only then killings in the name of religion, caste, creed, nationality, race, sex and colour will stop. Only when you start believing in the equality of every human being, do you start treating everyone with respect. This in turn wins you the respect of people and the love of God.

14.

Bahu<u>t</u>aa Bola<u>n</u> <u>Jh</u>a<u>kh</u>a<u>n</u> Ho-Ay.

Vi<u>n</u> Bolay Jaa<u>n</u>ai Sa<u>bh</u> So-Ay.

"To speak too much and babble is useless.

Even without our speaking, He knows everything."

(Ang 661)

The omnipresent omnipotent eternal Creator knows everything that's happening to you in your life. He makes provision for your food even before you are born. He, who ensures that you get your food even before you are born through your mother's milk, will always take care of you. He does not let even the birds sleep empty-stomach. Be genuine in your prayers and adopt an attitude of thanking your Creator for all that you have, for all that He's bestowed upon you. He not just holds you in your bad days but also shows you the way. At times, the bad days are a precursor to the good days. Just keep faith and be patient. He knows everything and will take care of you, no matter what.

15.

Birthee Ka<u>d</u>ay Na Hova-Ee Jan Kee
Ar<u>d</u>aas.
Naanak Jor Govin<u>d</u> Kaa Pooran
Gu<u>nt</u>aas.

*"The prayer of the Lord's
humble servant is never offered
in vain.
Nanak takes the strength of the
Perfect Lord of the Universe, the
treasure of excellence."*

(Ang 819)

Many of us feel that we do not get
enough results. We keep struggling
through life, working and toiling hard,

without tangible results. I would recommend them to try "Prayer Power". When you pray, you are before the most powerful supreme Force that is capable of doing anything. That Force can put wind in your sails and guide you to the right path. The Giver is always ready to give, its only you who needs to know how to knock the door. Do not pray asking for things. When you kneel before God assuming that He will give you good things, it is like expecting a return on investment. It is pure business not prayer. Pray with all your love and devotion. Be deserving of receiving, for when you are ready to receive, you shall receive. So whenever you feel that the results are not commensurate with the efforts put in by you, thank the Almighty for giving you an opportunity to prove yourself, then pray that His blessings be with you in your future endeavours – and then just get down to the execution of the work. See wonders happening for yourself.

16.

Kabeer Ka-Udee Ka-Udee Jor Kai
Joray Laa<u>kh</u> Karor.
Chal<u>t</u>ee Baar Na Ka<u>chh</u> Mili-O La-
Ee Langotee <u>T</u>or.

*"Kabeer, the mortal gathers
wealth, shell by shell,
accumulating thousands and
millions.*

*But when the time of his
departure comes, he takes
nothing at all with him. He is
even stripped of his loin-cloth."*

(Ang 1372)

The only thing worth earning in this
world is the karma of good deeds,

because that alone outlives everyone and everything. When one dies, one lives in other people's good memories. Just reflect and you will realise that there are so many people, from family or friends or work, etc., who might have left a lasting impression on you forever. Some of them might no more be around, but you still miss them for the good they might have done to you and the good times spent together. That is a way of making yourself immortal. You may see statues of once extremely powerful world leaders. But do you even bother to look at it twice? Not if they have genuinely done something for the people. On the other hand are so many people who create their statutes in our hearts and whenever we see something good we are reminded about them. The best way to immortalise oneself is to immortalise oneself in someone's good memories.

The times that we do not spend with our family and our near and dear ones is the time that's wasted. Work should be a means to an end and not the end itself – never forget that. Never put the cart before the horse. Whatever you are working for is temporary. So live your life – go out for walks, smile, love, laugh, cry, feel and most importantly, spend time with your family.

17.

Jaa Rah__naa Naahee Ai__t Jag __Taa Kaa-
I__t Gaarab Han__dhee-Ai.

*"Since one is not destined to
remain in this world anyway,
why should he ruin himself in
pride?"*

(Ang 473)

Pride and vanity blinds us. It gives us
a false sense of things and gives us a
distorted existence. We stop seeing
things the way they are. Break the
barriers set by vanity and pride and
step out to this world, the real world,
where things are beautiful, if you
have the eye to see the beauty. The

mighty Ravana, who was such a learned Brahamana and a devout Shiva bhakt, was also defeated, because of pride. Because of the boons given by Shiva, he thought he could not be killed. But the Giver of everything gives it only till you are deserving and He knows how to take things back if you misuse them. The riches in your life should make you humble. Always have the attitude of a giver, and that attitude only comes through genuine love. Love everyone who comes in your life, because love is one thing that instantly builds connection between two people, without even saying a word.

18.

Bhand Jammee-Ai Bhand Nimmee-
Ai Bhand Mangan Vee-Aahu.
Bhandahu Hovai Dostee Bhandahu
Chalai Raahu.
Bhand Mu-Aa Bhand Bhaalee-
Ai Bhand Hovai Bandhaan.
So Ki-O Mandaa Aakhee-Ai Jit Jameh
Raajaan.
Bhandahu Hee Bhand Oopjai Bhandai
Baajh Na Ko-Ay.

"From woman, man is born;
within woman, man is
conceived; to woman he is
engaged and married.
Woman becomes his friend;
through woman, the future

generations come.
When his woman dies, he seeks
another woman; to woman he is
bound.
So why call her bad? From her,
kings are born.
From woman, woman is born;
without woman, there would be
no one at all."

(Ang 473)

Respect womenfolk. God chose women to give birth to his creation. Women are special. It's their delicate nature that makes us believe that they are weak. In fact, women are emotionally and psychologically stronger than men. A man who keeps the womenfolk in his life, like mother, sister, wife happy, is bound to succeed, because in tough times, he draws upon their psychological support.

There is no difference between men and women in the Sikh religion. To ensure equal status for women, the Gurus made no distinction between the sexes in matters of initiation, instruction or participation in *sangat* (holy fellowship) and *pangat* (eating together). Guru Amar Das disfavoured the use of the veil by women. He assigned women to supervise some communities of disciples and preached against the custom of *sati*. Sikh history records the names of several women, such as Mata Gujri, Mai Bhago, Mata Sundari, Rani Sahib Kaur, Rani Sada Kaur and Maharani Jind Kaur, who played important roles in the events of their time.

Women are God's most precious creation, because it is through them that He chose to carry the creation forward. A woman holds the key to creation. Never let her be sad. Women are closest to being a creator.

19.

Naanak Kahee-Ai Kis Handhan
Karmaa Baahray.

*"O Nanak, how shall I tell them
this? Without the karma of
good deeds, they are only
destroying themselves."*

(Ang 147)

Its Karma that makes or breaks us.
We are all so intricately and invisibly
connected that our every action or
inaction has some implication
somewhere. So be careful in your
actions. A hole that you dig for others
might become your grave in no time.

Be good to others to beget good from others. No action or inaction is without a consequence so choose them wisely.

20.

Man Tan Arap Taj Laaj Lokaanee.

"Dedicate your mind and body to Him; stop living to please others."

(Ang 737)

It's your life. God is the giver and you are the author of your life. This thing called "life" is between you, the created and God, the Creator. It's no one else's business what you do with it. Whether you want to be a painter, a singer, a sportsman, just do it. Your limited time here was given to you not to please others or to be what others want you to be. Think about the way you would want your life to be. Is it the way you want it to be? No? Then take instant action and make amends to your life to give it a direction you want. Pray to God that so that He may bestow you with his blessings and strength while you strive to shape your life the way you want it to be, and just forget about what others will think about you. Whatever be it, there always will be someone out there to criticise you. So just think of yourself and what you want to do with your life and do it!

21.

Dookh Tisai Peh Aakhee-Ahi
Sookh Jisai Hee Paas.

"Tell your troubles to the One who is the Source of all comfort."

(Ang 16)

The most comforting cushion in the Universe is the name of God, provided you are ready to believe in Him. Belief has the power to move the mountains. Believe in Him and surrender to His will, and as you do so, talk to your troubles and inform them that they are around only for a short while, because the source you draw your strength from is on His way to help you. While you do so, believe in your own words. And see the wonders for yourself!

22.

Maan Na Keejai Sara̲n Pareejai Karai
So B̲halaa Manaa-Ee-Ai.
*"Do not be proud; seek His
Sanctuary, and accept as good
all that He does."*

(Ang 612)

Arrogance and ego are like cancer. It
creeps in without you realising it and
if not tended properly and timely, it
kills the body in which it is. How to
get rid of arrogance? Take the name
of God. Appreciate the beauty,
magnificence and grandeur of nature.
Look at it – it's been here before you

were around and it shall be here after you are gone. You are not here forever. This beautiful thing called life, will someday come to an end. Once you realise this, you will let go of arrogance. The realisation that we are not here forever makes us humble and that humility brings peace and happiness, because of the warmth that you spread all around yourself. If good happens well – nothing like it, but if it does not happen, don't be disappointed. It means that the Almighty has better plans for you and you are on your way to realise them. Just be aware, conscious, honest and conscientious, rest the Almighty will take care of.

23

Kar Updays Jhirhkay Baho Bhaatee
Bahurh Pitaa Gal Laavai.
Pichhlay A-Ogun Bakhas La-Ay
Parabh Aagai Maarag Paavai.
*"His father teaches him, and
scolds him so many times, but
still, he hugs him close in his
embrace.
Please forgive my past actions,
God, and place me on Your path
for the future."*

(Ang 624)

God is always giving, provided you are
deserving of receiving. Like a father,
He may only to make you strong, put

you through testing times, so that you develop wings strong enough to fly. He knows our vision is limited. He keeps giving signals for us to choose the right track. Only we should have the understanding. And how to develop the understanding? Meditate. Try to build a connection with Him. The path in front of you will start getting clearer. And when you start seeing clearly, never regret the past. You can never change the past, but nothing can stop you from starting change now and building a better future. Someday your present and future will become your past. Think over it. The situation you are in may be a result of past actions or inactions. Whatever be it, all you can do is change its course, today itself. Never let the bad past control or influence your present or future. If you keep looking behind while walking, you will either fall down or slow down. So in life, keep looking forward, the direction in which you are moving. And while doing so, invoke the blessings of God by surrendering to His will and regularly praying before Him.

24.

Hukmay Aavai Hukmay Jaavai Hukmay Rahai Samaa-Ee.

"*By His Command we come, and by His Command we go; by His Command, we merge in absorption.*"

(Ang 940)

The command of the Supreme is something that makes the universe work. There is something magical about the way everything functions, isn't it? True that the flower, buds and grows according to certain scientific principles, but who laid down those principles in the first place. Why are we born after 9 months and not 12 months? Why was earth at such distance from sun that we could survive here? All these cannot be explained by science. Spirituality begins where science ends. It's a realisation of the wondrous plan that makes us spiritual. And it is that marvellous plan that decides who does what. Not that one should be complacent. But don't take failures too seriously, because that failure is also a lesson that He wanted to teach you. So make your failures your best teacher, and don't fret too much over it – because in the end, when His command comes, all, the successful ones and the not so successful ones have to depart. So live your life till you are here.

25.

Oo<u>th</u>a<u>t</u> Sova<u>t</u> Har Sang Pahroo-Aa.
Jaa Kai Simra<u>n</u> Jam Nahee Daroo-Aa.

"While rising up, and while
lying down in sleep, the Lord is
always with you, watching over
you.
Remembering Him in
meditation, the fear of Death
departs."

(Ang 196)

This is a powerful line. Repeat this
during the day and feel the power of
the words. We all are children of that
Supreme Being. He looks after us all
day long and even when we are

sleeping in the night. The story of young Prahlada is a testimony to this fact. He was a strong devotee of Vishnu from his mother's womb. His father, Hiranakashipu was given a boon from the Gods that he could not be killed by anyone born out of a man or an animal, during the day or night, inside or outside the house. Hiranakashipu did not like his son, Prahlada's devotion to Vishnu, to the extent that when Prahlada did not pay heed to him to stop worshipping Vishnu, Hiranakashipu tried to kill him, his own son. He tried to kill Prahalada by crushing him under elephants, by throwing him in a room full of snakes and by placing him in the lap of his sister Holika, while she was in burning fire, since she was given a boon that she could not be burnt. But the young Prahlada kept chanting Vishnu's name who saved him everywhere. Finally, Vishnu appeared as Narsimha (half man and half lion) and killed Hiranakashipu at the entrance of his home during the dusk, thus nullifying Hiranakashipu's boon. The moral of the story is that one should be unwavering in his belief in God and God will always be there to help you. When you think there is no way you can be saved, God finds out a way to save you, and if that way cannot be found, He creates a way to help you. There is nothing to be afraid of. Nothing is bigger than Him and you are His child. So don't be afraid.

26.

Bha-ee Paraapat Maanukh Dayhuree-
Aa.

Gobind Milan Kee Ih Tayree Baree-
Aa.

"This human body has been
given to you.

This is your chance to meet the
Lord of the Universe"

(Ang 12)

Out of all species, He made you a
human being. You could have been a
tree, a horse, sea, a mountain or
anything else – but He gave you a

human form, the form that is intelligent and conscious. This was to understand the greatness of the Supreme Being and to be a provider to the ones in need. In whatever we do, we should always extend a helping hand to the ones in need and be a strength to the weak. Only then we come close to God. Remember, every weak person or a person in need who comes to you for help is an opportunity God has provided you to come close to Him. So while you are in human form, do good deeds, only then will you be close to God.

27.

Paarbarahm Para<u>bh</u> Ayk Hai <u>D</u>oojaa
Naahee Ko-Ay.
Jee-o Pind Sa<u>bh</u> <u>T</u>is Kaa
Jo <u>T</u>is <u>Bh</u>aavai So Ho-Ay.
*"There is only the One Supreme
Lord God; there is no other at
all.*

*Soul and body all belong to
Him; whatever pleases His Will
comes to pass."*

(Ang 45)

God merely created humans, its
humans who created religion.
Otherwise the universal religion is
humanity. Similarly God is one. It is

this realisation which will eradicate many ills like inequality, terrorism, etc from the face of the earth. We are subject to such ills because we think we are different from others.

One story that one cannot miss here is that of Bhai Kanhaiya ji. Bhai Kahaiya ji was a kind hearted person from a very young age and he was the water bearer in Guru Tegh Bahadur Ji's army. He used to tend the injured army and gave drinking water to them. One day the injured Sikh soldiers went to Guru Tegh Bahadur Ji and complained that Bhai Kanhaiya ji was giving water to injured Mughal soldiers as well. This, they complained, helped them to regain lost strength, which they used to fight against the Sikhs. Bhai Kanhaiya ji was called to the Durbar and Guru Ji asked him whether he was serving water to the Mughals, who were their enemy. Bhai Kanhaiya ji accepted that he was serving water to the Mughals, but he said that he saw no enemy in them. He said he saw human beings in them, same as everyone. Hearing this, Guru Ji smiled and turned to the Sikhs who came complaining and told them that Bhai Kanhaiya ji has correctly understood the teachings of Sikhism, which teaches equality of all mankind.

It is the same spirit of the universe that is in me that runs in you and in everybody. So we are all a part of one big family, called humanity. Think about it.

28.

Baho Chintaa Chitvai Aap Na
Pachhaanaa.
Dhandhaa Karti-Aa An-Din Vihaanaa.
*"The mind is distracted by great
anxiety; no one recognizes one's
own self.*
*Occupied with their own affairs,
their nights and days are
passing away."*

(Ang 159)

One habit through which we sabotage
our own success is worrying. This is
this habit that is absent in most
productive and successful people. Life
is a live show, not a staged play. Take

risks, feel the adrenaline rush and use your nervousness to your advantage. What if Michael Jackson or Shah Rukh Khan settled with comfortable and paying job? Their creative juices would not let them settle. They neither would have achieved the greatness which they have achieved, nor would they be happy or satisfied in the work that would be doing. Every one of us has a divine purpose to achieve. Take a break. Realise that and start doing that. While you get to doing it, nerves will try to get the better of you. Nervousness is a powerful energy. Channelize it to your advantage. It's like fire at the end of a rocket. It used properly, it can help propelling the rocket to great heights. It's a two edged sword. You need to know how to use it to your advantage. So stop worrying and start living.

29.

Su<u>kh</u> Mai Baho Sangee <u>Bh</u>a-
Ay <u>Dukh</u> Mai Sang Na Ko-Ay.
Kaho Naanak Har <u>Bh</u>aj Manaa
An<u>t</u> Sahaa-Ee Ho-Ay.

"In good times, there are many
companions around, but in bad
times, there is no one at all.
Says Nanak, vibrate, and
meditate on the Lord; He shall
be your only Help and Support in
the end."

(Ang 1428)

Look around yourself and you will
find that most of the people cling on
to you because of your position. If the

position goes, those people will also go. The ones who stay are family and real friends. One of them who always stays with you is the Almighty. Yes, you have the Supreme Being as your family and closest friend. Make Him your pillar of support by constantly reminding yourself that He is standing behind you and will always watch your back.

30.

Too Kaahay Doleh Paraa<u>n</u>ee-
Aa <u>T</u>u<u>dh</u> Raa<u>kh</u>aigaa Sirja<u>n</u>haar.
Jin Pai<u>d</u>aa-Is <u>T</u>oo Kee-Aa So-Ee <u>D</u>ay-
Ay Aa<u>dh</u>aar.
"Why do you waver, O mortal
being? The Creator Lord Himself
shall protect you.
He who created you, will also
give you nourishment."

(Ang 724)

He started caring for you even before
you were born. He gave you the safety
and warmth of your mother's womb
and nourishment through her milk.

There is absolutely nothing that should worry you, because He will always be there for you. So before starting your day, repeat this line five times. Feel a new you inside you, who is more robust, more stable and more reliable in trying times.

31

Bin Pareetee Bhagat Na Hova-Ee Bin
Sabdai Thaa-Ay Na Paa-Ay.
*"Without love, there is no
devotional worship. Without the
Shabad, no one finds
acceptance."*

(Ang 67)

An empty prayer just bounces back
from the ceiling. Your prayer should
be filled with love and devotion for
that Supreme Being. Do not
underestimate the prayer power. It is
something that connects you to the
Almighty. You can do wonderful
things with your prayer power,

provided you do it with love and devotion.

Manufactured by Amazon.ca
Bolton, ON